This Journal Belongs To

Manufactured by Amazon.ca
Bolton, ON

36806651R00068